The Moonflower

Dedicated to every child who ever asked "why?"

—Peter and Jean Loewer

Published by
PEACHTREE PUBLISHERS
1700 Chattahoochee Avenue
Atlanta, Georgia 30318-2112
www.peachtree-online.com

Text © 1997, 2019 by Peter Loewer
Illustrations © 1997, 2019 by Jean Loewer
First trade paperback edition published in 2004
Revised edition published in 2019

Jacket illustration by Jean Loewer
The illustrations were rendered in acrylic.

Printed in October 2018 by RR Donnelly in China
10 9 8 7 6 5 4 3 (hardcover)
10 9 8 7 6 5 4 3 2 1 (trade paperback)
HC ISBN: 978-1-56145-138-8
PB ISBN: 978-1-68263-101-0

Library of Congress Cataloging-in-Publication Data

Loewer, H. Peter
The moonflower / Peter Loewer ; illustrated by Jean Loewer. —1st ed.
p. cm. Summary: A brief look at some of nature's nocturnal behavior including the blooming of the moonflower, how moths drink, how bats "see," and how vines climb.
ISBN 1-56145-138-X
1.Moonflower—Juvenile literature. 2. Nocturnal animals—Juvenile literature. 3. Night-flowering plants—Juvenile literature. [1. Moonflower. 2. Nocturnal animals. 3. Night-flowering plants. 4. Night.] I. Loewer, Jean, ill. II. Title.
SB413.M65L63 1997 574.5—dc20 96-35976 CIP

The Moonflower

Peter and Jean Loewer

PEACHTREE
ATLANTA

When the Sun has set in the West…

...but the sky is still too bright for most stars to shine, the buds on the moonflower vine are closed tight. A bumblebee that cannot find the way to his underground home curls up in a flower to wait for dawn.

Bumblebees live in underground nests made of grasses and moss and are usually found in abandoned homes of mice and other small animals. Bumblebees make honey, but instead of storing it in combs, they make little pots that are kept in the nest. In the bright daylight, their compound eyes can see landmarks like open fields, small ponds, or dead trees, which help guide them back to their nests. At nighttime, the light from the Moon and stars is too dim for flying, so they rest overnight until the break of dawn when they head back home. Bumblebees only sting when threatened, and if left alone, are harmless companions in the garden.

Crickets do not actually sing, but a male cricket can make a friendly chirp by using the covers of its forewings like a violin, drawing one wing cover across the other. This chirping is usually meant to attract the female crickets in the area. If you count a cricket's chirps for 15 seconds and then add 40 to that number, you will know the approximate temperature in degrees of Fahrenheit. For Celsius, count the number of chirps for 25 seconds, divide by 3, and add 4. Crickets are often kept as pets in households across the world.

It's not really dark yet, but people turn on house lights, children park their bicycles at the back door, and crickets in the yard begin to sing.

Bats now wake from their daytime sleep, ready to swoop and glide, catching insects in the gathering darkness. The fireflies of summer will soon begin to send their flashing codes, shining like flying sparklers.

Bats use a kind of radar to see in the dark. They find their way by making high-pitched squeaks that echo off of night-flying insects, trees, and other objects. Their very large ears pick up these echoes and guide the bats to their prey and away from harmful obstacles. Because their wings can bend, bats are also better flyers than birds. Contrary to classic nursery rhymes, bats cannot get stuck in people's hair looking for bacon. They also pollinate flowers, eat bothersome insects, and help to spread seeds.

Fireflies, or lightning bugs, use a blinking tail light to communicate with each other. The male firefly flashes a special code that only the female firefly of the same species understands. The female firefly waits a few seconds before sending out its own series of flashes. A firefly's glow is produced by a chemical called luciferin, located in a small light organ at the tip of its abdomen. Unlike an electric light, there is no heat produced by the light of a firefly.

The summer Moon rises to the song of a mockingbird and the stars shine in the purple twilight. Fireflies begin to flicker. A nighthawk silently glides across the darkening sky in search of insects to eat.

On this warm summer night, the twining moonflowers begin to open, like a movie in slow motion. Wider and wider the petals unfurl under the Moon's silvery light.

Vines climb in many ways. Moonflowers grasp with tendrils and wind their stems around fences or branches. Some vines twine to the left, but moonflowers twine to the right.

Moths have a great sense of smell but do not have noses like you or I do. Moths detect odors and aromas by using their fine, feathery antennae. These antennae, or feelers, react to scents released into the night air by flowers that only open their petals at night or during a late and cloudy afternoon. Moth antennae are important to their sense of balance. If a moth injures or loses its antennae, it becomes lost and cannot fly. Moths are very beautiful insects. Some moths are as large as saucers, but a few are so small they're called micromoths. There are about 12,000 species of moths in America, but only 725 butterfly species.

The perfume of the moonflowers floats out on the warm night air. Suddenly the hawk moths appear, drawn by the sweet fragrance of the blossoms. The hawk moths flit from flower to flower, their wings blurred with speed.

Many different insects delight in feeding at night-blooming flowers, but the whir of a hawk moth's wings and the speed of its flight scare other insects away from the moonflowers. While flying among the flowers, the moths pick up pollen and it falls on the blossoms like golden dust.

A moth has a very long, hollow tongue called a proboscis. Moth tongues are often as long as their bodies, but are usually tightly coiled to reduce drag and help them fly faster. Moths can generally unwind their tongues until they resemble a thin soda straw. This allows them to plunge their tongues deep into a flower in search of nectar. In the world of flying insects, most people love butterflies because they fly by day. As a result, they know far less about moths and do not appreciate how very effective they are as flower pollinators, especially for night-blooming plants.

Owls, like other nocturnal animals, are more active by night than day. Although their eyes are far more sensitive to light than human eyes, owls can see clearly in very dim light because of a layer of special cells at the back of their eyes. These cells act like tiny mirrors that double the amount of light an owl needs to see with. Because owls cannot roll their eyes around in their heads like we do, they must move their heads from left to right to get a good view.

An owl calls and swoops low over an open field. A mouse runs to hide in the shrubbery thicket. The Moon climbs higher and higher, and the moonflowers continue to lift their blossoms to its glowing light.

By four o'clock in the morning, a soft glow appears in the East. Suddenly everything is hushed and silent. The hawk moths have flown away to hide from the light of day. They rest in the bushes and trees, blending in with the bark or sleeping in the curl of leaves. The Moon begins to set and the Sun soon rises. The moonflowers wilt in the early morning sunlight, but new buds are waiting to open the following night.

By the time a moonflower wilts, the process of forming seeds has already begun. Although the petals have fallen away, new seeds will grow in the body of the flower. Pollen grains from the stamens of other moonflower vines have moved to a new flower's pistil by clinging to night-flying insects. The pollen fertilizes the flower so that our world will always have moonflowers to enjoy.

After moonflower petals dry and fall away from the base of the flower, the part that remains will grow larger and form a new seedpod. In a few weeks, the pods will dry out and turn dark brown. If you live where the winters are above freezing, the pods may eventually split open as well, allowing many new seeds to tumble out and eventually grow into new moonflower plants.

The mourning doves coo and the robins sing. An alarm clock buzzes and the kitchen light comes on. The sky grows brighter and brighter.

The hawk moths, the bats, and
the budding moonflowers will
sleep through the day, waiting
for the night to come again.
Then the bats will swoop and
the hawk moths will soar and
new moonflowers will open,
their trumpets unfurling to the
song of the mockingbird and the
whir of the hawk moth's wings.

Nocturnal animals find dark places to rest or sleep during the day. Moths fold their wings and sit silently, hidden underneath a leaf or clinging to a shaded branch. Bats spend the day in natural caves, abandoned buildings, or even attics. Owls sleep in tree hollows or find silent places in the woods, abandoned thickets, or nearby parks. When the sun sets, these animals will once again come out to explore their nighttime world.

Planting a Moonflower

Moonflowers are very easy to grow. Soak the seeds in warm, not hot, water for a day and a night before planting. Soaking weakens the outer seed coat and helps the seed germinate and grow. The next day, plant three seeds in a three-inch-wide peat pot; plant three to make sure at least one seed germinates. Add enough water to a mix of clean potting soil so the mix is moist but not wet.

Put the pots in a warm place (around 65° to 70°F, or 18° to 21°C), and make sure the soil stays moist but not wet. You may cover the pots with a piece of plastic wrap. Do not put the pots in the hot sun.

The seeds will germinate and poke up leaves in three to five days. Remember to water the plants and keep them inside until the outside garden soil is warm and there is no danger of frost.

Then pick a spot outside that will get full sun at least half the day. Plant the peat pot and its moonflower vine in a hole that will contain the whole pot. You can also grow the plant in a large clay pot (6", or 15cm, wide or more). Make sure you provide something for the plant to climb upon—strings, stakes, a trellis, or a fence will do.

As soon as the days are hot and the nights are warm, your vine will begin to grow with great speed. It can easily grow up to 10' (3m) or more in a season. Keep your moonflower plant well-watered, and give it some liquid fertilizer every three weeks, following the package directions.

Moonflower seeds can be bought from most large garden centers or ordered through the mail from a seed catalog. While they are winter-hardy perennials, they are grown annually in most of the US. The species of moonflower that you can plant at home is called *Ipomoea alba*, but there are other white-blossoming plants found in America's fields and wastelands besides moonflowers. Not to be confused with the moonflower, *Datura stramonium* is a very dangerous and very poisonous plant. Daturas have ill-smelling leaves and sharp thorns. They bloom with a white, nocturnal flower called an Angel's Trumpet or a Devil's Trumpet. Daturas should be avoided if found in nature. Moonflowers, too, can be poisonous if ingested.

Words to Know

Abdomen (p. 12): The hindmost section of an *insect's* body. (In humans, the abdomen is the part of the body between the chest and hips.)

Antennae (p. 16): Flexible, feeler-like projections on the head of an *insect*, such as the *hawk moth*.

Bat (p. 11, 27): A *nocturnal*, winged animal with a mouselike, fur-covered body. Bats at rest hang upside down, gripping branches or cracks in rocks with their feet.

Bud (p. 7, 23): A small bump on a plant stem that grows larger with age and eventually turns into a leaf, flower, or leafy shoot.

Bumblebee (p. 7): A large black bee with yellow markings that makes a pleasant buzzing sound as it flies. Bumblebees carry *pollen* from one flower to another so the flowers can produce seeds.

Butterfly (p. 16, 19): An *insect* that hatches from an egg and becomes a caterpillar. Upon reaching its adult state, it flutters through the air with beautiful and often brightly colored wings. Butterflies are amongst the most beloved *insects* in the world and fly during daytime.

Celsius (p. 8): A widely used, international measure of temperature outside of the United States.

Compound eye (p. 7): A sight organ made up of many single eyes crowded close together. A *bumblebee* has two compound eyes, one on either side of its head.

Cricket (p. 8): A common *insect* that is often found outside on summer nights. Cricket songs are soft and high pitched.

Fahrenheit (p. 8): The common measure of temperature in the United States. Water freezes into ice at 32° Fahrenheit and boils at 212° Fahrenheit, or 0 and 100° *Celsius*.

Fertilizer (p. 23, 28): A manufactured chemical, like phosphorous or a natural substance like horse manure, that is mixed with soil to improve plant growth.

Firefly (p. 11–12): A soft-bodied beetle, sometimes called a lightning bug, that flies about on summer nights and glows with a flashing yellow light to attract mates.

Forewing (p. 8): Either one of the two front wings on a four-winged *insect*.

Germinate (p. 28): To develop and grow. With enough light, warmth, and water, seeds will grow and send out shoots and roots.

Hawk moth (p. 16, 19, 23, 27): A hairy, medium-to-large *moth* with a long *proboscis*. The hawk moth family includes some of the fastest fliers of all *moths*.

Insect (p. 11–12, 16, 19, 23): A small, invertebrate animal that crawls or flies and as a larger adult has three pairs of legs and one or two pairs of wings. Houseflies, *bumblebees*, and *butterflies* are all insects.

Luciferin (p. 12): A light-emitting compound found in both plants and animals. Luciferin glows but without producing heat, so it's known as cold light. This compound is used by lightning bugs when they blink on summer nights.

Mockingbird (p. 12, 27): A medium-sized gray-and-white bird with a slender, down-curved beak. It usually sings from high, open perches, and it imitates phrases from other birds' songs.

Moonflower (p. 15–16, 19–20, 23–24, 27–28): A climbing *vine* in the morning glory family with heart-shaped leaves. The moonflower's large white blooms that open in the evening are *pollinated* by night-flying *insects* like the *hawk moth*.

Moth (p. 16, 19, 27): A flying *insect* similar to a *butterfly*, often with beautifully colored wings, but generally flies at night and hides during the daytime.

Mourning dove (p. 24): A gray-brown bird with a small head and a long pointed tail. Its mournful song, "coah, cooo, cooo, coo," is often heard in late evening or early morning.

Mouse (p. 20): A small, furry animal, known as a rodent, that has rounded ears and a long furless tail. The most common species is the house mouse.

Nectar (p. 19): A sweet fluid, produced by flowering plants, that attracts *insects*, like bees or ants, and other animals, like bats or hummingbirds, to help with pollination. Bees collect nectar to make honey.

Nighthawk (p. 12): A slim-winged gray-brown bird that is *nocturnal*. Nighthawks feed on *insects*.

Nocturnal (p. 20, 28): Active at night.

Owl (p. 20, 27): A *nocturnal* bird with large eyes and with plumage so soft that it can fly almost without a sound.

Petals (p. 15–16, 23–24): Modified leaves that surround the reproductive parts of a flower. They are often brightly colored or have different shapes to attract pollinators like bees.

Pistil (p. 23): The female part of a flower that contains the ovules, or future seeds. *Pollen* must reach the pistil for seeds to form.

Pollen (p. 19, 23): Fine, powdery, usually yellow grains that are produced by the male part of a flower. Pollen must join with the ovules (this is called pollination) for future seeds to form.

Pollinate (p. 11): The act of moving *pollen* from one flower—or part of a flower—to another so new seeds can be produced. Many creatures carry *pollen*, including bees, bats, birds, wasps, and ants.

Proboscis (p. 19): The long, slender mouthpart of an *insect*, used like a soda straw to move food to the *insect's* stomach.

Robin (p. 24): A common red-breasted thrush often seen walking about looking for worms on lawns. Its clear and pleasant song includes sounds like, "tyeep" and "tut-tut-tut."

Seedpod (p. 24): A structure produced by plants that holds seeds, which eventually *germinate* and result in new plants. Peaches, apples, and milkweed pods hold seeds for future generations.

Stamen (p. 23): The male part of the flower. It is made up of a stalk with a sac at the tip where *pollen* grains grow.

Tendril (p. 15): A threadlike part of a climbing plant that is used for support. Tendrils twine around objects and hold on like gripping fingers.

Thicket (p. 20, 27): An area of dense growth made up of small trees, bushes, or shrubs that are growing closely together.

Vine (p. 7, 15, 23, 28): Generally, a weak plant stem that reaches for the sun using various *tendrils* for support as it climbs. If no support is found, vines sometimes creep along the ground in search of other stems to climb.

Wing cover (p. 8): The front pair of wings in many *insects* that have developed into covers. These covers are often beautifully marked and colored, and they fold over to protect the flying wings.